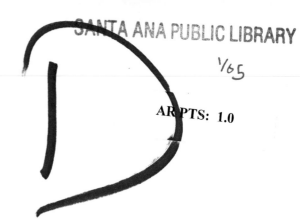

Inventions That Shaped the World

CURRENCY

PATRICIA K. KUMMER

Franklin Watts
A Division of Scholastic Inc.
New York • Toronto • London • Auckland • Sydney
Mexico City • New Delhi • Hong Kong
Danbury, Connecticut

Photographs © 2004: A Perfect Exposure/American Numismatic Association: chapter opener montage, 24; Art Resource, NY: 5 (Erich Lessing), 12 (Scala); Bridgeman Art Library International Ltd., London/New York: 22 (Hamburg Kunsthalle, Hamburg, Germany); Brown Brothers: 32, 47; Corbis Images: 68 (Ed Bock), 66 (Jon Feingersh), chapter opener montage, 17 (Chris Hellier), 64 (James Leynse), 25 (Francis G. Mayer), chapter opener montage, cover center right, 30 left, 43, 70–71 spots (Francoise de Mulder), 61 (Alan Schein), 6 (Paul A. Souders); Folio, Inc.: cover bottom left (Don Hamerman), cover bottom right, 52 left (TG MacMillan), 52 right (Eric Poggenpohl); Index Stock Imagery/ThinkStock LLC: 57; North Wind Picture Archives: 15, 34, 36, 38, 45; Peter Arnold Inc./Leonard Lessin: 30 right; Photo Researchers, NY: 19 (Jack Fields), 8 (Jeff Greenberg); PhotoEdit/Bill Aron: 63; Sovfoto/Eastfoto: cover top right, chapter opener montage, 18 (New China Pictures), 60 (Xinhua); Stock Montage, Inc./Tom Neiman: 55; The Image Works: 51 (Archives), 56 (Bob Daemmrich), cover center left, chapter opener montage, 27, 70 spots (HIP-Topham); Woodfin Camp & Associates/Jonathan Blair: cover left center, chapter opener montage, 28, 70-71 spots.

Cover design by Robert O'Brien and Kathleen Santini
Book production by Jeff Loppacker

Library of Congress Cataloging-in-Publication Data

Kummer, Patricia K.
    Currency / by Patricia K. Kummer.
        p. cm. — (Inventions that shaped the world)
Summary: Describes the invention of currency, a country's official unit of money; its history, and the impact it has had on modern culture.
Includes bibliographical references and index.
        ISBN 0-531-12341-3 (lib. bdg.)   0-531-16734-8 (pbk.)
1. Money—Juvenile literature. [1. Money.] I. Title. II. Series.
    HG221.5.K85 2003
    332.4′9—dc22   2003016309

CONTENTS

WHAT IS CURRENCY?

Cattle, shells, feathers, stones, salt, grain, iron, bronze, copper, silver, gold, coins, and paper notes. All of these items have been used as *currency* since about 6000 B.C. Staters, cash, wampum, thalers, yen, dollars, pounds, greenbacks, yuan, pieces of eight, euros. These are just a few of the names people have used for their currency during the past three thousand years. If currency has had all these

The shekel (above), an ancient form of currency in the Middle East, is now Israel's official unit of currency.

names and has been made from all those materials, then what exactly is currency?

Definition and Features of Currency

Simply stated, currency is the official unit of *money* used in a country. It can be dollars, pounds, euros, or shells. As long as the unit of money is accepted as the *medium of exchange*, that unit can be currency. This means that people agree on the kinds of coins, paper money, or shells that will be used for purchases of goods and services.

Besides being a medium of exchange, currency sets a standard of *value*. It lets people know how much things are worth. For example, if fans know how much a ticket to a

Shoppers can easily see the price, or standard value, for each produce item.

baseball game costs, they can figure out how much money they will need to purchase tickets for their entire family. Another example of currency as a standard of value would be the amount a person makes or charges as an hourly wage. If plumbers earn $30 an hour, then they will make $240 on a job that takes eight hours.

A third feature of currency is that it can be stored or saved and have lasting value. In other words, the worth of the currency will be the same during a long period of time. An allowance of $10 a week can be placed in a wallet. The following week the $10 is still worth the same as it was the week before. If milk were currency, however, it would have to be drunk or quickly used to buy something else before it spoiled. Milk cannot be stored for a long period of time and keep its value.

The fourth feature of currency is that it provides a *standard for deferred payment*. Currency becomes an accepted way to settle a debt. This means that people don't have to be paid at the end of each hour or each day. Employers promise to pay workers at the end of a week or after a two-week period. In turn, workers can purchase groceries or clothing and charge them to their credit card. They are promising to pay for these goods from the money they will get from their employer.

It's easy to see that currency *circulates*, or flows, between people and businesses as they buy and sell goods and services. In fact, *currency* can be traced back to the Latin word *currere*, which means "to flow" or "to run." If much of this

By giving change back to a customer, the clerk (above) helps currency circulate.

description of currency sounds like a definition of money, it is. *Currency* and *money* are often used interchangeably.

Inventions and Currency

Because currency plays such a major role in daily life, it's hard to believe that at one time currency did not exist. Without currency, how did people buy goods? How were they paid for their work? The invention of currency seems like one of those things—like the wheel and writing—that just had to happen for people and civilization to progress.

An invention usually arises from a need or from a desire to do something more easily or to make life better. Someone with imagination (an inventor) begins to think about making a product or developing a process (an invention). Work on an invention can take years. Sometimes inventions occur when two or more people, such as the Wright brothers, work together. Other inventions have developed in separate parts of the world at about the same time or at different times. This has happened because people in various parts of the world experienced the same needs. In the years before speedy transportation and instant communication, similar inventions or steps in an invention occurred independently in different places.

An invention usually develops as a result of an earlier invention or process of doing something. In the early 1800s, for example, Eli Whitney used the idea of interchangeable parts to develop the process of mass production. In this way, he was able to fill an order of ten thousand muskets in two years for the U.S. government. About a hundred years later, Henry Ford invented the assembly line to mass-produce Model T cars. These automobiles were made with interchangeable parts. The development of modern currency—coins and paper money— also relied on earlier inventions and processes.

Inventions Affect Daily Life

If an invention is truly useful, as the automobile proved to be, it becomes an important part of daily life. When this happens, improvements are made to the original product.

Advances sometimes also occur in how the product is made. What has been true of the automobile and other mechanical inventions is also true of modern currency. For example, the production method for coins has changed from when the first coins were struck in the 600s B.C. The same is true of paper money. In addition, checks, credit cards, and debit cards, as well as coins and paper money, are now considered to be currency.

Today almost every person, young and old, uses currency in some way each day. A child might use coins or paper money to buy an ice cream cone. An adult might write a check to pay for car insurance. Currency is also important to countries. Almost every independent country has its own currency—from the afghani in Afghanistan to the zloty in Poland. Other countries share a common currency, such as the euro or the West African franc. Because travel and trade throughout the world are so important, the currency of one country can usually be exchanged for the currency of another country. The old saying "Money makes the world go 'round" is still true in the early 2000s. Today more than ever, currency affects daily life and the life of governments around the world.

BARTER AND EARLY CURRENCY

Modern currency in the form of coins was not invented until the 600s B.C. How did people conduct business before that time? For thousands of years, people didn't need money. They lived off the land by hunting, fishing, and gathering nuts and berries. Early people made clothing from the skins of animals they hunted. They used mud, branches, and grasses to build homes. Each family took care of itself.

The Barter System

As the world's population grew, some groups became better than others at hunting or at fishing. One group might exchange part of its fish catch for an equal value of meat or animal hides from another group. This kind of exchange or trade is called *barter*. In the barter system, goods and services are directly traded for other goods or services. No money of any kind—coins, paper money, or shells—is used. In the barter system, as in a currency or money system, people have to agree on the value of the goods traded. For example, one animal skin might equal ten fish. When there were only a few items that people had or needed, barter worked well.

Then about ten thousand years ago, people began to settle on the land. They began to grow crops and to raise cattle. They lived together in villages. Over hundreds of years, people

Bartering in a European marketplace (above) determined the value of goods.

began to develop special skills. For example, some crafted wooden or metal tools for farmers. Others made clay pots for storing or cooking food. By specializing in one job, people now had a need for goods they did not make or grow. On certain days, people brought their goods to a marketplace in the village. At other times, people from several villages would set up a market at a crossroads or at a place along a river. Bartering took place in markets throughout the world.

SILENT BARTER

Not all barter took place in marketplaces and face to face. Sometimes one group of people needed goods from people who were their enemies or who spoke another language. In those cases, the first group placed their trade goods at a prearranged spot and then retreated into the woods or behind a hill. Then the second group placed the amount of goods they had for trade and likewise retreated. If the value of goods left by the second group was all right, the first group took them and went home. If the goods were not of acceptable value, the first group would remove some of their original goods and retreat again. This process would go on until both groups were satisfied that they had made a good trade.

Although people now had more goods to barter, the bartering system had become harder to use. Barter works well only as long as everyone involved has goods or services that others need. If a farmer wanted to barter wheat for a clay pot, he would have to find someone with an extra clay pot who wanted wheat. If the pot maker didn't need wheat, the farmer was out of luck. Another drawback to barter was that it took time. First, farmers and crafters had to find someone who wanted their goods. Once a good match was made between the goods to be traded, the two people had to agree on the value of the goods. Perhaps two bushels of wheat equaled one bushel of corn; two bushels of corn might equal a spear; a spear might equal three clay pots. In this method of accounting, three clay pots equaled four bushels of wheat. Remembering these equivalencies and calculating them became more difficult as more and more items appeared in the marketplace. There was no standard of value on which to base all items. No one item was used as currency.

Early Commodity Currency Develops

To simplify the trading process, people in different parts of the world began to use various objects as currency or money. Objects such as cattle, salt, grains, and beans are known as *commodity currency*, or commodity money. These objects have value in and of themselves. For example, cattle can reproduce; cows give milk. In bad times, cattle can be slaughtered for meat and the hides used for clothing, shoes, and other leather goods.

About 6000 B.C., cattle became the first objects used as currency. Other goods were assigned values in relation to

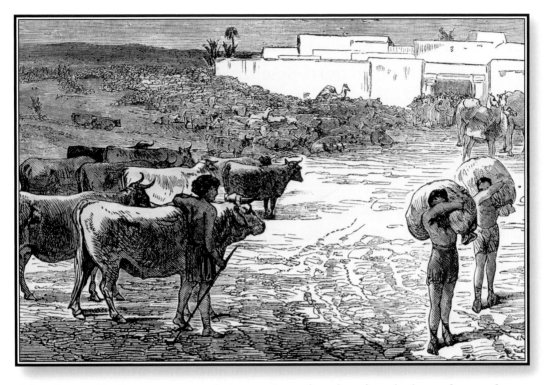

A herder waits for an appropriate number of sacks of grain in exchange for his cattle.

cows or oxen. Cattle filled three of the basic features of currency. They served as a medium of exchange, had a standard of value, and could be stored. In parts of Africa, cattle are still used as a measure of wealth among some ethnic groups. However, the cattle are not used as money.

Although cattle were an excellent standard of value and could be stored, they sometimes proved to be a difficult medium of exchange. If a coat or a piece of furniture was worth only part of a cow, the cow's owner could not cut up the cow. The value was in the whole cow that could give milk and reproduce calves, not in the cow's meat that would have to be quickly cooked and eaten.

Other commodity currencies, such as salt, beans, and grains, were good media of exchange and had standards of value. Bars of salt and bags of grain and beans could easily be divided for small purchases. Salt was used as currency across much of North Africa. The Roman Empire paid its soldiers in bars of salt. Rice became a form of currency in Asia; workers in the ancient Middle East were often paid in barley; cacao beans had value in ancient Mexico; wheat remained a currency in many parts of the world until the mid-1800s. Storing or saving salt, grain, and beans was not easy, however. When salt got wet, it disappeared. Over a period of time or during bad weather, grain and beans could rot and lose their value.

Other Early Currencies

Early traders and governments continued to look for longer-lasting forms of currency. About 1400 B.C., people in China were the first to use cowrie shells as currency. In fact, the Chinese character for money originally depicted a cowrie shell. Later, the use of cowrie shells as currency spread to India and many parts of Africa. Cowries are smooth, hard shells found in the Indian and Pacific oceans. Cowries came in many sizes and colors. Different values were assigned to them by color and size. Because of their hardness, cowries were impossible to *counterfeit.* People could not make fake

Cowrie shells were a convenient medium of exchange for early peoples.

cowries. Nor could cowries be *debased*. The shells could not be chipped or cut into parts. Only whole cowries had value.

In the A.D. 1500s, Native Americans in North America also began using shells as currency. Their currency was wampum—small beads drilled from clam shells. The beads were strung together and then sewn on to buckskin belts.

Many shapes and sizes of metal have been used as currency in several parts of the world. As early as 3000 B.C., Egyptians were using copper rings as currency. By 1850 B.C., ingots, or lumps, of silver were used in Mesopotamia, which is now Iraq. Gold ingots were used throughout the ancient Mediterranean world. Bronze coins shaped like hoes, knives, and spades were first used in China during the 700s B.C. By the 200s B.C., these tool-shaped coins were replaced by round coins with a square hole in the middle. These coins were called *cash*. Cash could be strung together and worn around the neck or carried on a stick. As early as the A.D. 1200s, people throughout West Africa used manillas, bracelets

Three stages of Chinese currency—cowrie shells, tool-shaped coins, and cash

THE WORLD'S HEAVIEST AND LIGHTEST MONEY

People in the South Pacific have had the world's heaviest and lightest money. On Yap Island, huge stone wheels with a hole in the middle (left) served as currency until late in the 1900s. Some of the stones weighed more than 500 pounds (226 kilograms) and were as much as 12 feet (3.5 meters) across. People on the island of Santa Cruz collected crimson feathers, or dyed them that color, and then glued them to a cloth belt. The belt was then wound up and wrapped in palm leaves.

made of copper or brass, for currency. Until the 1950s people in Liberia used hammered and twisted iron rods as currency.

Although shells and metal money lasted longer than grain

and salt, large amounts of them were hard to carry around. They were heavy. Metal money had another drawback. The weights of ingots and other objects were not consistent or standard. Each time a purchase was made, the merchant had to weigh the metal money. The purity of the silver, gold, or bronze was another problem with early metal currency. This made it difficult to know the true value of the money. Many of these problems were solved when the first metal coins were made.

WHO INVENTED MODERN CURRENCY?

No one person is credited with inventing modern currency—coins and paper money. Because modern currency has been developing from the 600s B.C., many people throughout the world have played a role in the stages of currency's invention. However, the names of only a few of these people are known. Most of the inventors worked for kings, emperors, or other rulers. They received no special recognition; their names were not recorded for history. In some cases, rulers themselves advanced the idea of modern currency.

The Kings of Lydia

In the small Asia Minor kingdom of Lydia, in what is now southwestern Turkey, a dynasty of kings built a wealthy country. Lydia's wealth was based on trade and on making and selling perfumes and cosmetics. Instead of bartering or using commodity currency, Lydian traders and merchants used coins. Between 640 and 630 B.C., King Ardys of Lydia

The scene above depicts the luxury and wealth of King Croesus's court. Visitors presented Croesus with gifts as payment for taxes and fines.

had the world's first coins *minted*. Minting is making coins from metal.

Lydia's coins were called staters and were made of *electrum*. This metal is a natural mixture of gold and silver. Electrum is sometimes called white gold. By minting and using coins, the kings and their kingdom became even richer.

"Rich as Croesus"

The most famous and richest of the Lydian kings was Croesus (595–546 B.C.). Before coming to the throne in 560 B.C., Croesus had traveled to Greek cities along the west coast of Asia Minor. People in these cities were minting silver coins that competed with Lydia's electrum coins. When Croesus returned from his travels, he told his father, King Alyattes, that Lydia should also mint silver coins. Alyattes began minting silver coins as well as electrum. The coins minted under Alyattes had a standard weight. Each stater equaled 168 grains of wheat.

When Croesus became king, he added to Lydia's wealth as well as his own by expanding trade. He also brought the Greek cities in Asia Minor under his control. In addition, Croesus minted the first gold coins in 550 B.C. and continued minting silver ones. He ended the practice of making electrum coins. Thus, Croesus introduced the world's first *bimetallic currency system*. Lydia made

Though difficult to see on this well worn Lydian stater, the lion's head emblem meant that the king guaranteed the value of the coin.

both gold and silver coins. These coins were also called staters. Twelve silver staters equaled one gold stater. Several smaller gold and silver coins were also minted. In that way, Lydians had coins of several values from which to purchase goods at the market.

Croesus's own fortune was huge and well known

THE PATRON SAINT OF COIN MAKERS

The Catholic Church has many saints. Some of them are patron saints, or special saints, to whom workers in various occupations look for help. Saint Eligius (A.D. 590–660) is the patron saint of coin makers, coin collectors, and metalworkers. During the A.D. 600s, Eligius became master of the mint in what is now Paris, France. A *mint* is a place where coins are made. In addition to *striking* coins for King Clotaire II, Eligius made

a golden throne inset with precious gems. In 639, Eligius became a priest and the next year was named bishop of Noyon-Tournai. After his death, he was canonized for his good works with the poor and for freeing slaves. Saint Eligius is honored on December 1, a special feast day in the Catholic Church. A famous work of art (left) by Petrus Christus in 1449 shows Saint Eligius weighing gold in a goldsmith shop.

throughout the Mediterranean world. As the amount of gold in each stater decreased, Croesus received the extra gold. Even today, people with a great deal of money are said to be as "rich as Croesus." Croesus turned out to be Lydia's last king. In 547 B.C., the army of the Persian Empire captured the capital of Sardis and conquered Lydia. Cyrus, the king of Persia, had Croesus put to death in 546 B.C. Lydia became part of Persia. However, Lydia's coinage system spread throughout other lands near the Mediterranean Sea. Croesus's bimetallic system was used in Europe and the United States until the 1800s, when most of the world went on the *gold standard*.

The Father of the Dollar

About two thousand years after the first coins were minted, Count Stefan Schlick and his family ruled the town of Jáchymov in the kingdom of Bohemia. This town is now part of the nation called the Czech Republic. About 1516, miners discovered silver in Joachimsthal, a valley near Jáchymov. Three years later, Count Schlick began minting large silver coins. At first he called the coins *Joachimsthalers* after the valley. In German, *thal* means "valley." This name was soon shortened to *thalers*. For about one hundred years, almost 12 million thalers were minted in Jáchymov.

During that time, the use of thalers spread to most of

This thaler coin was minted in 1662 for Duke Christian Ludwig of Brunswick, Germany. His initials appear under a crown on the horse, which was his family's symbol. At the bottom of the coin, workers are shown mining silver used to make the thaler.

the kingdoms in Europe. They were called talleros in Italian, daalders in Dutch, dalers in Swedish, and finally dollars in English. Some countries even called their own coins *thalers*. Some scholars estimate that more than ten thousand

Spanish coins were minted in various shapes and sizes and with different symbols. Each coin had its own value.

kinds of thalers were minted between 1519 and 1900.

Perhaps the most famous thalers were Spanish pieces of eight, also known as Spanish silver dollars. Minted in Spain and in Spain's American colonies, they were the main coins in the thirteen American colonies. In fact, Congress established U.S. currency based on Spanish dollars, which continued to circulate in the United States into the 1800s. A piece of eight could be broken into eight pieces, or bits. Each bit equaled twelve and a half cents. Two bits equaled twenty-five cents, a quarter of the whole coin's value. In the United States, people still refer to twenty-five cents and the quarter coin as "two bits."

In 1792, Congress made the dollar the official unit of currency in the United States. Today at least twenty countries, including Australia and Zimbabwe, use the term *dollar* for their official currency. They all use the same dollar sign ($) as the United States. This symbol is believed to have come from the design on the back of the old Spanish silver dollars. The design included two pillars crossed by a waving banner. Early dollar signs had two lines through them.

Johan Palmstruch—Early Father of Paper Money

Although paper money was first issued in China in about A.D. 800, the names and stories of the people involved are not

WOMEN ON THALERS AND DOLLARS

Although few women are featured on coins, one of the best-known thalers is the Maria Theresa (bottom left). This silver coin was first struck in 1773 in honor of Maria Theresa (1717–1780), the powerful empress of Austria. After her death in 1780, the thalers continued to be struck using the date 1780. Before the Austrian mint stopped making them in 1975, Maria Theresa thalers had spread far and wide. Coin specialists estimate that about 800 million Maria Theresa thalers were minted—all with the date 1780. For many years, these coins were the main currency in many North African and Middle Eastern countries.

In 1979, more than two hundred years after the first Maria Theresa thaler had been minted, the U.S. Mint struck the first U.S. coin to honor a woman. This was the Susan B. Anthony dollar (bottom right). Anthony (1820–1906) had spent most of her life working for women's right to vote. Unlike the Maria Theresa thaler, the Anthony dollar never became popular. Because of its size, people confused it with the quarter. Within a few years, the U.S. Mint stopped making Susan B. Anthony dollars.

known. Instead, two Europeans and an American are often called the fathers of paper money. The first was Johan Palmstruch (1611–1671). Some historians believe he was Dutch; others have him coming from the area of present-day Estonia and Latvia. Palmstruch had an interest and background in money and banking. He arrived in Sweden in the 1650s. With the permission of the Swedish government, Palmstruch set up the Stockholm Bank in 1656. In 1661, Palmstruch had the bank issue Europe's first printed paper money. The paper notes were printed in the denomination of 100-daler notes. People were supposed to be able to exchange them for a hundred silver dalers.

By 1667, Palmstruch's bank had issued too many paper dalers. The bank did not have enough silver to pay people who came to redeem their notes. The Swedish government found Palmstruch guilty of not properly managing the bank. Because he could not repay the people or the government, he was sentenced to death. His sentence was lowered to time in prison. Palmstruch was released in 1670 and died the following year.

John Law—Another Father of Paper Money

The Scotsman John Law (1671–1729) is also thought to be a father of paper money. His father was a goldsmith and banker. As a boy, Law was good at mathematics and worked at his father's bank. Later, he made his living as a

John Law introduced paper money to France, almost ruining the country's economy.

gambler before being convicted of a gambling-related murder in England. Law then fled to Holland and traveled throughout Europe, where he learned how banks in other countries worked. He had ideas for reforming banking through the use of paper money. He wrote about his ideas in *Money and Trade Considered with a Proposal for Supplying the Nation with Money* (1705). Law believed that by using paper money, more people would be put to work, and industry would grow. Law tried to get the governments of several countries to try his idea, but none wanted to use paper money.

Then, in 1716, the government of France allowed Law to set up the General Bank and to issue paper notes. At first the plan worked well. France's government was able to pay off its debts, and business boomed. By 1719, however, the bank had issued more notes than it had gold to back them up. People lost their money, and the bank failed. In 1720, Law fled France. Nine years later, he died a poor man in Venice.

Benjamin Franklin—Father of U.S. Paper Money

Sweden's and France's bad experiences using paper money kept many other countries from allowing notes to be issued. Benjamin Franklin (1706–1790), a printer and inventor in colonial Pennsylvania, thought paper notes should be used in the thirteen colonies. The youngest of

Benjamin Franklin (right) wanted Americans to use paper money.

ten children, Franklin learned to read as a helper in his brother James's printing shop. Eventually Franklin had his own printing and publishing business. Sometimes he printed money for the Pennsylvania colony on his printing press. In 1729, Franklin wrote the pamphlet *A Modest Enquiry into the Nature and Necessity of a Paper Currency.* Like Law, Franklin believed that paper notes would increase trade, encourage more people to go into specialized occupations, and make it easier for people to buy goods. However, the British government outlawed the use of paper money in the colonies.

During the American Revolution (1775–1783), the American government used Franklin's idea. The Continental Congress issued paper notes called Continental Currency, which were backed by silver and gold. By 1780, they had lost so much value that the government stopped issuing them. For many years, when referring to something of little value, Americans would say that it was "not worth a Continental." Nevertheless, after the American Revolution the idea and use of paper currency continued in the United States. The individual states issued their own paper currency. Eventually, the U.S. government also issued paper currency. Today Palmstruch and Law are almost forgotten. Franklin, however, is honored for his early work on paper currency by having his portrait on the hundred-dollar bill.

The Continental Congress issued more than $240 million in Continental Currency.

CHAPTER FOUR

MAKING COINS AND PAPER NOTES

Early commodity currency, shells, and metals had draw-backs. What was needed was a form of currency that had four particular features. First, it had to be light and easy to carry. In that way, people could have enough money with them to buy what they needed. Second, each piece of currency needed a standard value. In other words, each piece of currency would not have to be weighed for each use or purchase. Third, the currency had to be dividable into smaller units, so that people could make small purchases. Fourth, currency required an official seal or symbol to guarantee its value.

From ancient Lydia and China to modern Sweden, France, and the United States, the invention and develop-ment of modern currency have spanned hundreds of years

Workers perform the tasks that change raw metal into struck coins.

and thousands of miles. The invention of modern currency took place in two stages. First, coinage developed. Much later, paper currency was invented.

DEVELOPMENTS THAT HELPED THE INVENTION OF COINS

Before modern currency in the form of coins could occur, other processes had to be in place. People had to develop ways to remove copper, tin, silver, and gold from underground and from streams and rivers. Metalworkers had to develop methods of melting these metals. They then developed two other skills needed in metalworking. They invented ways to make certain metals stronger by making alloys. An alloy is a mixture of two or more metals. Also, through the melting process, they developed ways to remove impurities from the metals.

Invention of the First Coins

Most historians agree that the first coins came about because of a need by merchants, traders, and customers for a more reliable currency. By the 600s B.C., people were using varying weights of metal ingots—bars or other shapes of iron, bronze, copper, silver, and gold. Metalworkers backed by kings and other leaders developed what is now known as modern currency. However, no records exist of exactly when, where, and by whom these first coins were struck.

What is known is that the first coins were made between 640 B.C. and 630 B.C. in Lydia. They were made from small lumps of electrum. The electrum was softened by heating. Then, it was placed on a stone or hard metal slab called an anvil. Finally, the electrum was struck by a square punch hit by a hammer. This striking process is what made it a coin. Lydia's official currency, the stater, was oval in shape.

Changes in the Coining Process

Later, designs were struck into the coins through the use of metal dies. A design was carved into a die that was set into the anvil. Then, the soft metal was placed over the die and struck. The first designs were indented in the coins. In later coins, the designs stood out in relief.

By the 550s B.C., Lydia's coin makers were turning out gold and silver oval staters. Several denominations of staters were struck from whole staters to coins as small as 1/96th of a stater. The lion head, the symbol of Lydia's kings, was struck onto the front of each coin. The back of each coin had a symbol for its value. The symbols helped people who could not read to know the coins' values. Thus, the four requirements for currency had been met. The staters had an official seal that guaranteed their value. The currency came in coins of several sizes. Each size of coin had a standard shape and weight, and each

The first mints were in temples throughout the ancient Middle East and Mediterranean. At that time, people believed in many gods and goddesses. Each deity had its own temple. Kings and other leaders believed that temples were a safe place to make and to store coins. In addition, kings gave money to the priests of the temples. The priests in turn offered prayers for the king to the god or goddess of the temple.

coin had its value stamped on it. The staters were also small and easy to carry around.

Since the 500s B.C., many refinements and improvements have occurred in the coining process. The Greeks began minting round coins. When Persia (now called Iran) conquered Lydia, the Persians made gold coins stronger by adding copper to them. The Romans designed two dies hinged together. When the two dies were aligned with the blank metal between them, they could be struck. A design then appeared on both sides of the coin.

By the A.D. 900s in Europe, slowly cooled sheets of silver were pounded out until they were smooth. Blanks, the term for round pieces of metal before they become coins, were cut by hand and then struck. In the 1500s, screw presses and roller presses stamped the designs on blanks. Today, rolling presses flatten bars

Screw presses were used from the 1500s until they were replaced by steam-powered presses in the 1830s. With this type of machine, a large iron screw moved an upper die down toward a blank piece of metal that was positioned on a lower die. After the coin was struck, the screw raised the upper die.

Who or what turned the screw? In the first U.S. Mint in Philadelphia, harnessed horses turned the screw presses that made the new nation's first coins. Later, manpower turned these presses. A long iron bar was attached over the top of the screw. Heavy weights with leather straps were attached to each end of the bar. Two or more men on each end would pull the straps in one direction to turn the screw downward. After the coin was struck, they would pull the straps in the other direction to raise the screw and begin again. Another man sat in front of the screw press. He placed blank sheets of metal between the dies and removed the finished coins.

of metal into huge sheets of heated and then cooled metal. From these sheets, blanking presses punch out about 2,100 blanks a minute. Next, the blanks are pushed through an upsetting machine that upsets, or raises, a rim around the edge of each blank. Finally, coining presses stamp a design on both sides of the blanks, which are now coins. In spite of all the improvements and new

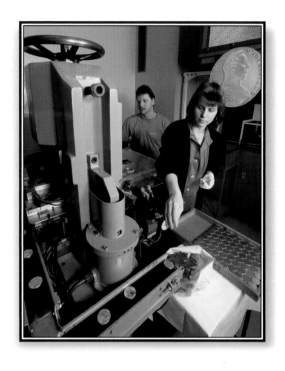

Machines and workers perform the same coin making tasks in modern mints throughout the world.

technology, the basic steps of coin making remain the same as in early Lydia—melting, cooling, and striking.

The Invention of Paper Currency in China

Just as commodities, shells, and various metals became inconvenient as currencies, so too did gold, silver, and copper coins. In China, about A.D. 800, merchants and traders were tired of carrying around the heavy coins, called cash. They also feared being robbed on their travels.

PAPER AND PRINTING

Two inventions had to take place before paper currency was possible. These inventions were paper and printing. Both inventions took place in China. Cai Lun is credited with inventing paper about A.D.100. He made it from a pulp of mulberry bark, hemp rags, old fishing nets, and water. The pulp was dried in thin sheets that could be written on. About A.D. 600, printing began when someone applied ink to carved wooden blocks.

They began depositing their coins with bankers who, in return, issued printed paper notes. The notes equaled the amount of cash coins. These notes could be exchanged at the merchant's hometown bank. Called "flying cash" or "flying money," these notes could fly away in a breeze. The notes were block-printed on mulberry bark paper using red and black inks.

About 1023, the Chinese government took over printing paper notes. Each note had a standard value and the seals of the emperor and his treasurer on them. They could be used on their own or exchanged for coins. The notes were larger than a piece of notebook paper. However, a 1,000-cash note weighed much less than the 8 pounds (3.6 kg) of 1,000 cash coins. In 1260, the Chinese government made paper money the only legal currency. All coins were called in. By the 1400s, the government had issued so much

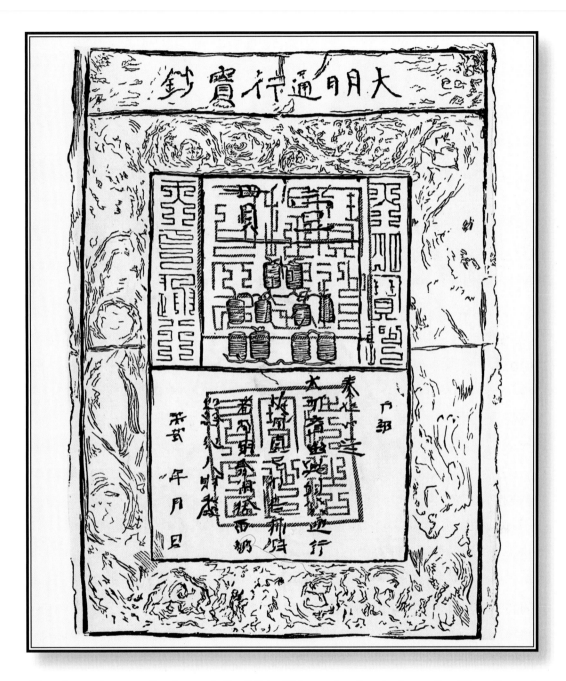

The characters on the lower left of this Chinese banknote from the Ming Dynasty (1368–1644) warns that counterfeiters will be punished.

paper money that it lost its value. By 1455, China had returned totally to coin currency. China did not issue paper money again until the early 1900s.

Paper Currency in Europe and America

In Europe, the development of paper money began in the late 1200s. European merchants and traders were experiencing the same problems that the Chinese had in the 800s. Bankers and goldsmiths in what is now northern Italy issued handwritten promissory notes and bills of exchange to merchants who deposited gold and silver with them. In the promissory notes, bankers promised to pay back the amount of the gold or silver deposited upon return of the note. Bills of exchange allowed merchants to trade in faraway countries without carrying their gold and silver coins with them. A bill of exchange said that one kind of currency would be paid in another kind of currency on a certain day and place.

Printed money did not appear in Europe until 1661. At that time the Swedish government was running short of copper, the main metal for their coins. The value of the copper coins was based on silver. Sweden's government decided to allow a bank to issue paper notes backed by silver. Within a few years, the bank had issued so many notes that they had lost value.

During the next two hundred years, other European gov-

When the Confederate States of America lost the Civil War in 1865, all Confederate currency became absolutely worthless.

ernments and governments in the Americas experimented with paper money. This usually occurred when supplies of metal for coins were low, especially during wars and revolutions. During those events, paper notes were not backed by gold or silver. During the American Revolution (1775–1783), Congress issued Continental Currency. For a few years during their revolution (1789–1799), the French had paper notes called assignats. During the U.S. Civil War (1861–1865), the Confederacy and the U.S. government each issued paper currency. The U.S. dollars were called greenbacks because they were printed with green ink. Most of these currencies could not be exchanged for an equal amount of gold or silver. By the late 1800s, most countries had currency systems of coins and paper notes.

During the 1900s, people realized that if a government was strong and reliable, they could trust the value of its coin and paper currency. The coins themselves did not have to be made of gold or silver, and the paper did not have to be exchangeable for gold or silver. In fact, by 1971, U.S. currency could no longer be turned in and exchanged for gold.

Most of the world's currency is now an alloy of metals such as copper, nickel, and zinc. In fact, some countries don't even mint coins. Because the minting process is so expensive, these countries use only paper currency.

THE ROLE OF CURRENCY

Many historians think that the invention and use of modern currency are the world's most important developments. Some of them think that modern currency improved life for most people and helped expand people's contacts around the world. Other historians feel that the use of modern currency has cut people off from real relationships with others. In addition, they believe that almost everything, including people's worth, has been reduced to a monetary value.

Effect on Trade

Currency was developed to make trade easier. Indeed, the use of coins and then paper did make it easier to buy and sell goods in the marketplace. By using currency, everyone involved in trade—farmers, craftspeople, factory owners, merchants—paid or was paid in coins or paper. In turn, all these people paid their workers and helpers in currency. Eventually, just about everyone took part in the circulation of currency.

Sometimes people had money left over after paying for food, clothing, and housing. They might invest the extra money in their own business or in someone else's business. Then, more jobs were available to produce more goods and services. Whole industries developed as a result of currency.

New Industries Develop

One of the first industries to develop was that of minting money. Miners obtained the metals for coin making. Artists and engravers cut designs into dies. Workers with strong arms and steady hands struck the coins. Other people kept track of how many coins were minted and where they were stored. Today, thousands of people around the world work in mints that produce millions of coins each day.

Banking is another major industry that developed. At first, banks provided a safe place to deposit gold and silver coins. Bankers issued promissory notes, bills of exchange, and letters of credit. These pieces of paper made it possible to exchange the currency of one country

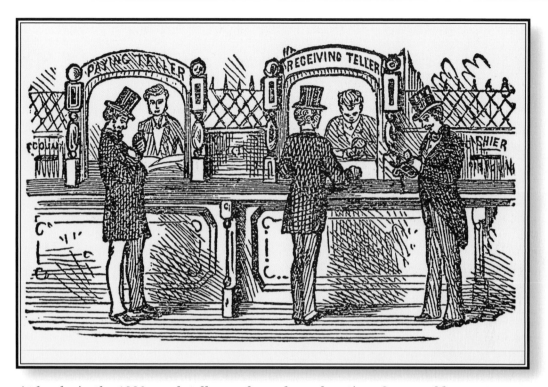

At banks in the 1880s each teller performed one function. One would accept money for deposits; another would take care of withdrawls.

for that of another without actually handling coins. This allowed merchants and traders to buy foods and goods not produced in their own countries. Traders also looked for new markets in which to sell goods from their own countries. Gradually, bankers began to issue paper notes that could be used in place of larger values of coins. Most of these banks were privately owned.

Governments and Currency

From the beginning, the minting of coins has been under government control. Governments have always taxed and

51

THE FEDERAL RESERVE BANK

The central bank of the United States is the Federal Reserve, called the Fed for short. It was established in 1913 to regulate the supply of U.S. dollars and their value. The Fed also balanced the competing interests of the country's many private banks. Today, the Fed is made up of twelve banks in major cities throughout the United States. It is run by a seven-member board of governors. The governors are appointed by the president of the United States and confirmed by the U.S. Senate. Alan Greenspan (bottom left) is the current chair of the Fed.

The Fed issues all paper money in the United States. Each denomination of bill has the words *Federal Reserve Note* printed on the top front. Each bill also has the name of one of the regional Fed banks printed in a seal on the front. The U.S. Bureau of Engraving and Printing in Washington, D.C. (bottom right), and in Fort Worth, Texas, prints all U.S. paper money for the Federal Reserve. It then ships the bills to the correct regional Fed bank, which in turn distributes the notes to other banks in the region.

fined their citizens. Before the invention of currency, citizens paid taxes and fines with goods—foods or manufactured products. With the coming of currency, governments took payments in coins. Governments could then pay their workers in coins.

During the past hundred years, governments around the world began to control the banks in their countries. Each major government set up a central, or national, bank for its country. Each country's paper currency was printed or issued from its central bank. The ability to coin and to print money has become one of the first things a newly independent country does. This shows that a country can stand on its own in the world.

Today, one of a government's biggest jobs is to maintain a good economy so that its currency maintains its value. If a country's currency loses value, it costs that country more to buy goods from other countries. In turn, the citizens of that country must pay more for imported goods. Governments are now involved with many other money-related issues, such as the cost of living, wages, and unemployment.

Effect of Currency on Everyday Life

Before the invention of currency, men, women, and sometimes children traded directly with the person who grew or made a product. They had to negotiate the value of the

COUNTERFEITING AND DEBASING CURRENCY

Counterfeiting, or passing off fake currency as real, began with the earliest currencies. Colored glass beads were used to create counterfeit wampum, which was made of clam-shell beads. Having so much counterfeit in circulation devalued the real wampum. Today the U.S. Treasury Department works constantly to make it difficult for counterfeiters to make and pass counterfeit bills. A special mixture of linen and cotton rag cloth is used to make the paper. The paper in turn has a watermark. Secret blends of inks are used to engrave the designs on the bills. In the late 1990s, the $5, $10, $20, $50, and $100 bills were redesigned. The portraits on the fronts were set off-center to the left. In 2003, the $20 bill (right) was redesigned again. The frame around President Andrew Jackson's portrait was removed. Shades of blue, green, and peach were added to the front of the bill. These and other changes made it harder to counterfeit the bills.

Other criminals debase currency—that is, they remove some of its value or add impurities to the original currency. For example, some early people who used cacao beans as currency would remove the bean from the pod and replace it with mud. In this way, they got the use

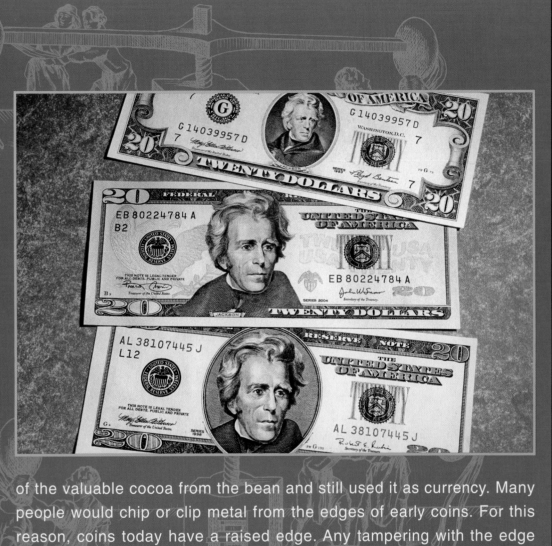

of the valuable cocoa from the bean and still used it as currency. Many people would chip or clip metal from the edges of early coins. For this reason, coins today have a raised edge. Any tampering with the edge is easily visible.

goods. Now, people buy goods in stores at set prices. They don't know who grew their food or who made their car. Although the spread of currency brings people in touch with foods, clothing, and cars made in other countries,

This customer may have written a check or used a credit card, or a debit card, to pay for her purchase.

NUMISMATICS

For hundreds of years, people have been interested in *numismatics*, or studying and collecting currency. The first book about coins was

written in China by Hung Tsun in 1149. At first numismatics was related only to coins. Now the term also includes studying and collecting paper money. After stamp collecting, the world's most popular hobby is numismatics. Some people try to collect a coin and a paper note from each country. Others specialize in the currency of one particular country. Still other numismatists look for coins or notes that have flowers, animals, or ships on them.

most people do not develop a close relationship with their local merchants.

Today, people are dependent on currency. Their time at work is valued in a unit of currency. They meet their wants and needs by purchasing goods and services with currency. From a packet of flower seeds for a small garden to a huge oil painting in the living room, everything costs money. This causes some people to become "money grubbers." They put in long hours at work to earn as much money as possible. If people lose their jobs and run out of money, they often feel worthless. Their self-worth is tied to the amount of money they have. For good or for ill, money has become the main necessity in life. Without it, people can't acquire the other necessities—food, water, clothing, housing, medicine.

People who live in a country that has a stable currency usually have opportunities to lead a good life. Not everyone becomes rich, but most hold jobs that pay enough to live well. They can pay their taxes, send their children to college, pursue sports and hobbies, and take vacations. Many average people even invest in the stock market. Today, the value of a country's currency is important to each of its citizens.

CHAPTER SIX

MANY NEW FORMS OF CURRENCY

Currency circulates, or flows, through the economy as people make purchases, pay taxes, deposit and withdraw money from the bank, or give money as a gift. The currency of one country also flows into the economies of other countries. By the early 2000s, much of this circulation was taking place without any physical coins or paper money. Again, the form of currency is changing. Bankers, merchants, and consumers are trying to develop more convenient kinds of currency.

Toward Plastic Currency

As early as the 1920s, department stores began offering charge cards to their customers. Some of these cards were made of cardboard paper; others were metal. Shoppers could

COMPUTERS AND CURRENCY

Computers made the increased use of checking accounts and the development of credit cards possible. Banks and large companies could store large amounts of information on computers. Through their computers, banks could keep track of deposit and withdrawal information. From this, the banks could determine how much credit a person should carry on a credit card. In turn, credit-card companies used computers to keep track of billing and payment information across the country. Before the development of computer technology, it was impossible to record and track this kind of information.

charge purchases and then pay the entire bill, usually within thirty days. Charge cards were convenient because people didn't have to carry so much cash—coins and paper bills—when shopping. These cards could be used only in the store that issued them.

MasterCard and VISA are the most widely used credit cards.

In the 1950s, Diners Club and the American Express Company issued the first plastic credit cards. These cards differed from the earlier charge cards in three ways. First, they were plastic. Second, they could be used at any restaurant, hotel, and store that accepted them throughout the United States. Third, because they were credit cards, payment of the entire amount was not required. However, if customers carried part of the bill over to the next month, they were charged an interest fee. In the 1960s, gasoline companies such as Shell, Mobil, and Gulf Oil also began offering credit cards to be used at their gas stations.

Checking Accounts and Bank Cards

With the increased popularity of charge cards and credit cards, more people also began using checking accounts. Instead of depositing money only in a savings account at the bank, people could also deposit money in a checking account. Then when it came time to pay the credit-card and charge-card bills, people would write a check for the exact amount to the department store or credit-card company and mail the payment. This was more convenient than standing in line at the store to pay the bill. Sending a check through the mail was also safer than sending coins and paper bills.

By the late 1960s, banking companies began offering

This young woman is paying for CDs with a check. Her bank will withdraw money from her checking account and give it to the merchant.

credit cards. They came out under the names of MasterCharge and BankAmericard. These cards are now known as MasterCard and VISA. Banks in other countries issued similar cards. Eventually, these cards could be used almost anywhere in the world—at restaurants, hotels, department stores, gasoline stations, grocery stores. Now, students at colleges and universities can charge their tuition and fees on credit cards. People can even use credit cards to buy a car.

During the 1990s the plastic debit card was developed. Debit cards are directly linked to a person's savings or

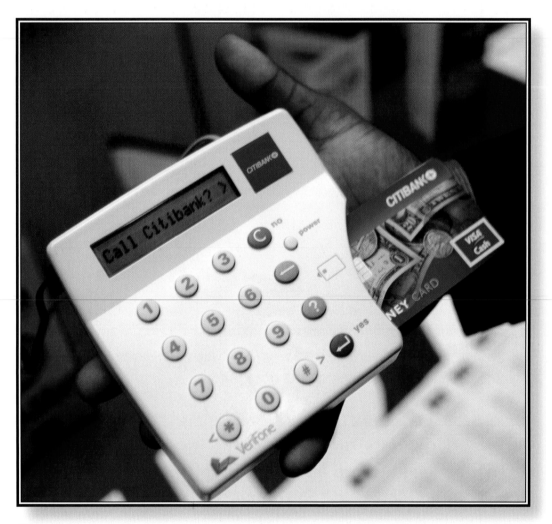

The smart card shown above has a certain amount of money recorded on its computer chip. With each purchase, an amount of money is subtracted from the card.

checking account. For example, when customers use their debit card to purchase groceries, the amount is automatically taken from their bank account and transferred to the grocery store's bank account. Also in the 1990s, smart cards became available in Europe. These plastic cards have an electronic chip that stores much information. For example, it can hold a person's bank-account and credit-card information. It also can allow people access to public phones and passage through tollgates on highways. In this way, people have to carry only one card and can totally forget about carrying cash.

Electronic Currency

Since the 1980s, government agencies and private companies have been paying their employees through direct deposit. This means that the paycheck is deposited electronically into an employee's checking account. Many companies, such as electric, gas, and telephone companies as well as credit-card companies, now offer direct payment of bills to their customers. In this process, the customer authorizes the withdrawal of a certain amount each month to the particular companies.

In the 1990s, making electronic payments through Internet bank accounts began. People can now set up an online account. It lists a person's bank accounts and all the companies that regularly bill the person. When bills come due, the

Sitting at her home computer, this woman is writing an electronic check to pay a bill through her Internet bank account.

person goes online and inputs the necessary information. Money is then sent from the person's bank account to the billing company's bank account.

"Cashless," Not "Currency-less"

Many historians and economists believe the world is moving toward a cashless society. This is probably true. More and more people are using plastic cards and electronic transfers to take care of business. However, the world is not becoming a "currency-less" society. The amounts dealt with in credit-card, debit-card, and electronic transactions are in units of currency. U.S. dollars, British pounds, Mexican pesos, and other currencies are still used as the media of exchange. These currencies still have a standard of value and can be used to defer payment. They can also still be stored.

Where they are stored marks the main difference for these new forms of currency. Instead of being present only in a wallet or in the bank, currency can now be stored on computers as information. The actual currency isn't seen or touched. In the future, physical dollars, cents, pounds, and pesos might no longer be printed or minted. As long as people trust that the value of currency is protected, its shape, size, color, or material doesn't matter.

New Currencies

At the same time that people were moving away from using coins and paper money, a new currency came into use. In 1999, twelve European countries (Austria, Belgium, Finland, France, Germany, Greece, Ireland, Italy, Luxembourg, the Netherlands, Portugal, and Spain) gave up their individual currencies and adopted the euro. In 2002, the new euro coins and bills went into circulation.

The famous windows and gateways on the front of euro notes represent openness among the euro countries.

French francs, German marks, Italian lire, and Spanish pesos stopped being official currency. The euro makes trade and travel easier among these countries. Currency in the twelve countries no longer has to be exchanged at various rates. The euro is regulated by the new European Central Bank.

Going beyond the euro, some economists would like to see a world currency. One advantage of this would be that all countries would have a common interest in keeping the world safe. As electronic technology expands into every corner of the world and into every home, a world currency might be possible someday.

CURRENCY: A TIME LINE

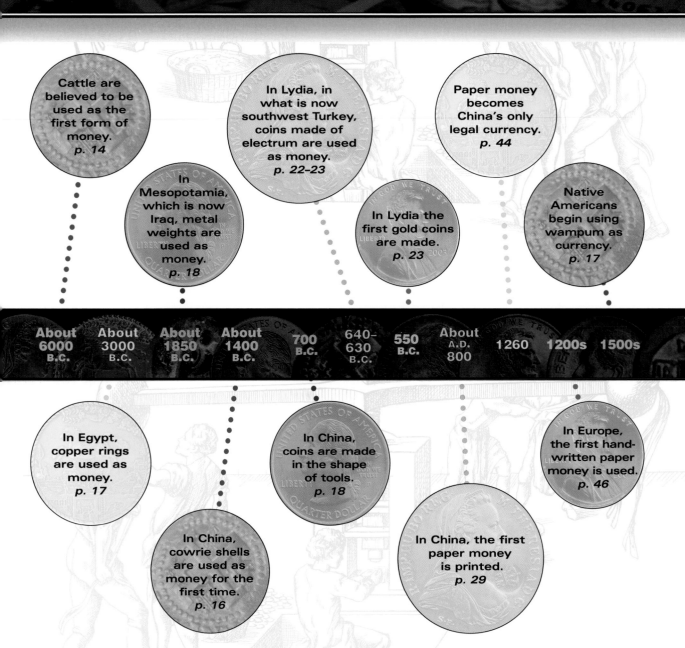

Cattle are believed to be used as the first form of money. *p. 14*

In Mesopotamia, which is now Iraq, metal weights are used as money. *p. 18*

In Lydia, in what is now southwest Turkey, coins made of electrum are used as money. *p. 22–23*

In Lydia the first gold coins are made. *p. 23*

Paper money becomes China's only legal currency. *p. 44*

Native Americans begin using wampum as currency. *p. 17*

| About 6000 B.C. | About 3000 B.C. | About 1850 B.C. | About 1400 B.C. | 700 B.C. | 640–630 B.C. | 550 B.C. | About A.D. 800 | 1260 | 1200s | 1500s |

In Egypt, copper rings are used as money. *p. 17*

In China, cowrie shells are used as money for the first time. *p. 16*

In China, coins are made in the shape of tools. *p. 18*

In China, the first paper money is printed. *p. 29*

In Europe, the first hand-written paper money is used. *p. 46*

70

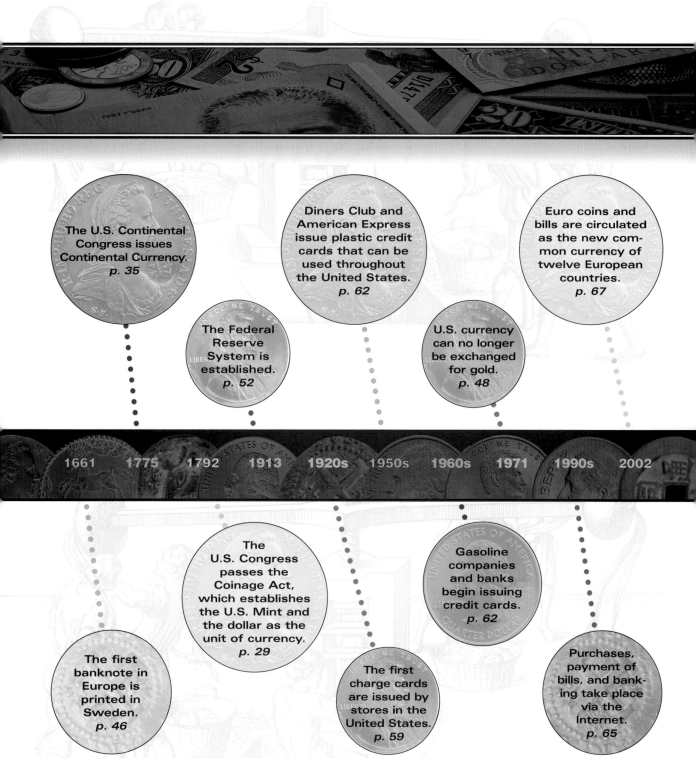

The U.S. Continental Congress issues Continental Currency. *p. 35*

Diners Club and American Express issue plastic credit cards that can be used throughout the United States. *p. 62*

Euro coins and bills are circulated as the new common currency of twelve European countries. *p. 67*

The Federal Reserve System is established. *p. 52*

U.S. currency can no longer be exchanged for gold. *p. 48*

1661   1775   1792   1913   1920s   1950s   1960s   1971   1990s   2002

The U.S. Congress passes the Coinage Act, which establishes the U.S. Mint and the dollar as the unit of currency. *p. 29*

Gasoline companies and banks begin issuing credit cards. *p. 62*

The first banknote in Europe is printed in Sweden. *p. 46*

The first charge cards are issued by stores in the United States. *p. 59*

Purchases, payment of bills, and banking take place via the Internet. *p. 65*

GLOSSARY

barter: The direct trading of goods and services for other goods and services without the use of money

bimetallic currency system: Currency system in which two kinds of metal coins, usually gold and silver, are used

cash: Early Chinese coins with a square hole in the middle; another word for coins and dollar bills

circulate: To flow among people, businesses, and banks

commodity currency: Goods, such as grains, cattle, and salt, that have value in and of themselves

counterfeit: To make a copy of a piece of currency for use as the real thing

currency: Coins and paper money that are in circulation; money issued by a government

72

debased: Lessened in value as a result of adding lower-quality metals or replacing materials

electrum: A natural metal that contains both gold and silver

gold standard: The currency system in which coins and paper money can be exchanged for their value in gold

medium of exchange: Items, such as coins, paper money, or shells, that a group of people agree have a certain worth or value

mint: To make coins from metal; a place where coins are made

money: A medium of exchange, such as coins and paper bills, for buying and selling goods and services and for paying debts

numismatics: The study and collection of currency

standard for deferred payment: A feature of currency or money that implies a promise of future payment for goods or services

striking: Stamping a design on a blank piece of metal, thus making it a coin

value: The amount that something is worth

TO FIND OUT MORE

Books

Allen, Larry. *Encyclopedia of Money.* New York: Checkmark Books, 2001.

Cribb, Joe. *Money.* New York: DK Publishing, 2000.

Giesecke, Ernestine. *From Seashells to Smart Cards: Money and Currency.* Chicago: Heinemann Library, 2003.

Video

Growing Up Well—Piggy Banks to Money Markets: A Kid's Video Guide to Dollar and Sense. Peter Pan Industries, 2002. A 27-minute video in DVD and VHS format. Includes materials other cultures use for money, how and where U.S. bills and coins are made, explanations of banking, checks, and credit cards.

Web Sites

The American Numismatic Association Programs for Young Numismatists

http://www.money.org/ynprograms.html

Web site for young coin collectors that includes a newsletter, a trivia game, information for earning Boy Scout and Girl Scout badges in coin collecting, and forms for scholarships, conferences, and awards.

Board of Governors of the Federal Reserve System

http://www.federalreserve.gov

Web site of the Federal Reserve with links to a map of the Fed's twelve districts and to each of the Federal Reserve banks and their museums.

Lake Region

http://www.lakeregion.com/news0101.htm

Web page that lists several money museums in the United States with phone numbers and basic information for each.

The U.S. Mint's Site for Kids

http://www.usmint.gov/kids/

This Web site leads to pages of games, cartoons, a time machine, and news about coins.

Welcome to Money Central Station

http://www.moneyfactory.com/kids/start.html

The area of the U.S. Bureau of Engraving and Printing Web site for kids with two sets of pages: one for children five to eight years old, the other for nine to thirteen year olds. Includes interactive displays, games, and fun facts, many of which deal with counterfeiting and anticounterfeiting features of the new U.S. Federal Reserve Notes. Macromedia Flash Player™ required for these pages.

Organizations

The American Numismatic Society
Broadway at 155th Street
New York, NY 10032
(212) 234-3130
info@amnumsoc.org

Bureau of Engraving and Printing
14th and C Streets, SW
Washington, DC 20228
(202) 874-3019

U.S. Mint Headquarters
801 9th Street, NW
Washington, D.C. 20220

INDEX

ABOUT THE AUTHOR

Patricia K. Kummer writes and edits nonfiction books for children and young adults from her home office in Lisle, Illinois. She earned a bachelor of arts degree in history from the College of St. Catherine in St. Paul, Minnesota, and a master of arts degree in history from Marquette University in Milwaukee, Wisconsin. Before starting her career in publishing, she taught social studies at the junior high/middle school level. Since then, she has written more than forty books on the United States and countries in, Africa, Asia, and Europe.

Ms. Kummer hopes that this book will help young people better understand how currency developed and continues to evolve, as well as the important role that currency plays in daily life and in the life of nations.